The Topsy-Turvies

Francesca Simon

Illustrated by
Emily Bolam

Orion
Children's Books

The Topsy-Turvies originally appeared in
The Topsy-Turvies first published in Great Britain in 1995
by Orion Children's Books
This edition first published in Great Britain in 2012
by Orion Children's Books
a division of the Orion Publishing Group Ltd
Orion House
5 Upper Saint Martin's Lane
London WC2H 9EA
An Hachette UK Company

1 3 5 7 9 10 8 6 4 2

Text © Francesca Simon 1995, 2012
Illustrations © Emily Bolam 1995

The right of Francesca Simon and Tony Ross to be identified
as author and illustrator of this work has been asserted.

ISBN 978 1 4440 0512 7

Printed in China

www.orionbooks.co.uk

For a complete list of Early Reader titles
by Francesca Simon and Emily Bolam
look at the back of the book.

For Miranda Richardson

Once upon a time there lived a family called the Topsy-Turvies.

The Topsy-Turvies always got up
at midnight.

They put on their pyjamas.

Then they went upstairs and
had dinner.

'Eat up, Minx,' said Mr Topsy-Turvy.

Minx juggled with the sausages.

'Clever girl!' said Mr Topsy-Turvy.

'Jinx, stop eating with your fork,' said Mrs Topsy-Turvy. 'You know that's for combing your hair. Please use your fingers and toes.'

'Could you pass the jam please,
Minx?' said Mr Topsy-Turvy.

Minx dipped her fingers in the jar
and hurled the jam at her father.

'Thanks,' said Mr Topsy-Turvy.

'Could you pass the whipped cream
please, Jinx?' said Mrs Topsy-Turvy.

Jinx flung a handful of cream at
his mother.

'Thanks, dear,' said Mrs Topsy-Turvy.

Then it was time for school.

After school they went to the park.

Then they played beautiful
music together,

and watched TV.

Afterwards they ate breakfast.

Then it was bathtime, and then
they all went to bed.

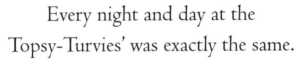

Every night and day at the
Topsy-Turvies' was exactly the same.

Until…

One afternoon a loud knocking
at the door woke them up.

'Who could that be at this time of day?' yawned Mrs Topsy-Turvy.

It was their neighbour, Mrs Plum.
'Oh dear,' said Mrs Plum.
'Were you just leaving?'

'No' said Mrs Topsy-Turvy. 'Why
would I go outside wearing my coat?'

'I'm sorry to bother you,'
said Mrs Plum. 'But I have to go out.
Could you look after little Lucy?
She's as good as gold.'

Mrs Topsy-Turvy was very sleepy,
but she liked helping others.

'Of course,' said Mrs Topsy-Turvy.
We'll be undressed in a minute.'

As soon as everyone was ready, they went next door to Mrs Plum's house.

'Thank you so much,' said Mrs Plum.
'Do make yourselves at home and have
something to eat.'

And off she went.

'Mum, why is Mrs Plum wearing clothes outside?' said Minx?

'Shh,' said Mrs Topsy-Turvy. 'Everyone's different.'

The Topsy-Turvies goggled at
Mrs Plum's house.

Nothing looked right.

'Poor Mrs Plum,' said Mrs Topsy-Turvy.
'Let's make the house lovely for her.'

The Topsy-Turvies went to work.

They fixed, they fussed, and they put
the room in apple-pie order.

That's better,' said Mr Topsy-Turvy.

'Careful, Lucy, don't put that apron
on, you'll get paint all over it,'
said Mr Topsy-Turvy.

'Lucy! Don't draw on the paper!'
said Mrs Topsy-Turvy.
'Draw on the walls!'

'Isn't she naughty?' said Minx.

'Not everyone can be as well behaved
as you, dear,' said Mrs Topsy-Turvy.
'Lucy, what a lovely picture!'

'I'm hungry,' said Jinx.

'So am I,' said Minx.

Mrs Topsy-Turvy looked
at the clock.
It was almost five.

'We might as well have breakfast,'
said Mrs Topsy-Turvy. 'Let's see what
food we can find in the bedroom.'

It took them a very long time to find
where Mrs Plum kept her food.

'What an odd house,'
said Mr Topsy-Turvy.

'How funny to eat in
the kitchen,' said Minx.

'Breakfast is under the table,'
said Mrs Topsy-Turvy.
'Don't forget to wash your feet.'

'What's for dessert?'
said Minx.

'Tomatoes,' said
Mr Topsy-Turvy.

'Yippee!'
said Jinx.

'But no tomatoes until you
finish your cake.'

'Do I have to eat ALL
my cake?' said Jinx.

'Yes,' said Mrs Topsy-Turvy.

Suddenly there was a noise
at the window.
It was a burglar.

'Hurray! We've got a visitor!'
shouted Minx.

'And he's coming through
the window!' shouted Jinx.

'Let's make everything lovely for our guest,' said Mrs Topsy-Turvy.

'Please, have something to eat,' said Mr Topsy-Turvy, throwing tomatoes at the burglar.

The burglar looked unhappy.

'Have some cake,' said Jinx, hurling his leftovers.

'No, have some of mine!' shouted Minx.

'Mine too!' shouted Lucy.

The frightened burglar escaped
as fast as he could.

'Why did he run off?' said Minx.

'I don't know,' said Mrs Topsy-Turvy.

Then Mrs Plum ran in.
'Is everything all right?' said Mrs Plum.
'I just saw a burglar jump out of
the window!'

'Everything's fine,'
said Mr Topsy-Turvy.

'You chased away a burglar!'
said Mrs Plum.

'Thank you so much. Goodness what
a mess he made!'

'What mess?' said Mrs Topsy-Turvy.

The Topsy-Turvies waved
goodbye and went home.

'Mrs Plum should have said thank you for
making her house so lovely,' said Minx.

'Never mind,' said Mrs Topsy-Turvy.
'It takes all sorts to make a world.'

Look out for more Early Readers by
Francesca Simon and Emily Bolam:

 **Runaway Duckling**

Where Are My Lambs?

 **Billy the Kid Goes Wild**

Barnyard
Hullabaloo

Mish Mash
Hash

Chicks Just
Want to
Have Fun

Moo Baa
Baa Quack

Meet
the Gang

Yum Yum

Rampage
in Prince's
Garden

Jogger's
Big
Adventure

The Haunted House of Buffin Street

Miaow Miaow Bow Wow

Look at Me